AF272115

THE INSPIRED CHOICE

Chronicles of Transformation
Beyond Imagination

Volume 1

Caroline Biesalski

The Inspired Choice

Chronicles of Transformation Beyond Imagination

Caroline Biesalski

Bibliografische Information der Deutschen Nationalbibliothek:
Die Deutsche Nationalbibliothek verzeichnet diese Publikation
in der Deutschen Nationalbibliografie; detaillierte
bibliografische Daten sind im Internet über http://dnb.dnb.de
abrufbar.

Verlag: BoD · Books on Demand GmbH, In de Tarpen 42,
22848 Norderstedt

Druck: Libri Plureos GmbH, Friedensallee 273, 22763 Hamburg

ISBN: 978-3-7597-2130-3

CONTENTS

FOREWORD BY BRIAN PROCTOR

It is with great pleasure that I write the foreword for The Inspired Choice: Chronicles of Transformation beyond Imagination. This book by Caroline Biesalski is not just a guide—it's a heartfelt invitation to step into your greatness, embrace your potential, and create a life of purpose and fulfillment.

In reading Caroline's work, I'm reminded of the timeless lessons my father, Bob Proctor, shared with the world. He often spoke of the power of choice and the responsibility we have to shape our own futures. Caroline embodies this philosophy, weaving personal stories, insights, and actionable strategies into a tapestry of inspiration. She reminds us that every decision we make is a step toward the life we're meant to live. Caroline's passion for helping others shine through every page. Her unique ability to connect with people and guide them toward discovering their true potential is evident in the transformative principles shared within this book. She takes readers on a journey—not just through her own experiences, but through the universal truths that empower us all to rise above limitations and embrace our inspired choices.

As you turn these pages, be ready to reflect, grow, and take action. Caroline's words are more than ideas; they are catalysts for transformation. She beautifully demonstrates that the secret to success lies not in external circumstances, but in the inspired choices we make every day.

I encourage you to immerse yourself in The Inspired Choice: Chronicles. Let it ignite your imagination, fuel your ambition, and guide you to live with intention. Caroline has truly created something extraordinary here, and I know it will make a lasting impact on your journey.

With gratitude and inspiration,
Brian Proctor

INSPIRED

In the beginning was the Word, and the Word was with God, and the Word was God. He was with God in the beginning. Through him all things were made; without him nothing was made that has been made. In him was life, and that life was the light of all mankind. -John 1:1-5, NIV

Replace the words "he, him" by Imagination. Read it again.

Imagination is the starting point of ALL creation. Napoleon Hill

"God gave you an imagination for a reason and this reason is: to use it!" Troy R Chadwick

CHOICE

As Bashar shares, "Everything is fundamentally meaningless." It is your free will to choose that gives you power and clarity—if you use this power wisely. Without duality, there can be no choice; everything simply *is.*

You have the power to assign meaning to things, and that meaning shapes your experience. To God, you mean the world. He gave you the ability to create meaning so you could pass it on to everything and everyone you encounter.

Are you mindful of your thoughts, words, and actions? They shape the choices you make today—and ultimately, the life you create.

TODAY

What conscious choice will you make today to inspire yourself and contribute to a better world for all of humanity?

1. THE JOURNEY BEGINS

From a young age, I was captivated by the magic of radio. When people asked me what I wanted to be when I grew up, my answer was simple: "One day, I want my own radio show." That dream was ignited in the late 1980s when I bought my first cassette player. I loved recording snippets from radio shows, creating my own playlists, and imagining myself as a radio moderator, playing my favorite music and interviewing fascinating guests.

But as much as I cherished this dream, I never dared to pursue it. Labels like "shy" and "introvert" held me back. I accepted these definitions of myself and acted accordingly. Speaking up in school felt like an insurmountable challenge, and even as I grew older, the fear of judgment and rejection kept me from expressing myself. Social anxiety led me to avoid people, events, and opportunities. I convinced myself that I wasn't wanted or invited.

Yet, deep down, I knew there was something more. Beneath the self-imposed limitations, I dreamed of being a journalist, an interviewer, or even a writer. My love for storytelling and connecting with others never truly faded.

In 2007, podcasts began to emerge with the rise of the iPod, and I was hooked. I carried my little silver iPod everywhere, listening to podcasts all day long. The format inspired me deeply, but I still didn't believe I could create something of my own. Instead, I pursued a different path, building a career in accounting, founding my own company, and managing a team of six employees. Despite my success, the dream of creating something meaningful lingered.

In 2023, during a transformative road trip from Los Angeles to Colorado Springs and back, I reconnected with myself. It was a courageous journey, one that pushed me to reflect on my path. On the night of December 12, 2023, I woke up at 3 a.m. with one word on my mind: *podcast*. I knew, with absolute certainty, that this was my moment to begin.

That same day, I recorded my first episode. The process was exhilarating yet daunting. I planned to alternate between solo episodes and interviews, but doubts crept in. Would people agree to be my guests? Could I overcome my fear of rejection? I reminded myself that if I never asked, the answer would always be no. So, I took the leap—and to my surprise, every person I invited said yes.

This was the birth of *Inspired Choice Today*. Guided by intuition, I trusted that podcasting was the right step for me. Starting in San Diego on December 12, 2023, my journey quickly gained momentum. As I write these words, I've recorded nearly 530 episodes in just 11 months.

This journey is more than a personal success story—it's a testament to the power of action and intuition. I want to share this story with you to show that if I can do it, so can you. Whether you dream of hosting a podcast, writing a book, or pursuing a passion, I hope this book inspires you to take that first step.

Let's embark on this journey together. Remember, every big success starts with a single inspired choice.

2. SETTING THE STAGE

With an external microphone, my computer, and BeeKonnected as recording platform, I had everything I needed to begin. The key was eliminating excuses. Technology wasn't going to hold me back. The real challenge was committing to the journey and trusting that I could do it.

The first step was to make a committed decision. I promised myself that I would record at least 50 episodes, no matter what. This mindset gave me a clear focus and eliminated the option of quitting. I reached out to friends and connections from 2023, inviting them to be guests as a way of giving back. To my surprise, everyone said yes - except for one exception.

Initially, I planned to alternate between solo episodes and guest interviews, but the enthusiasm of my guests quickly shifted the focus. Interviews became the backbone of the podcast, while solo episodes became rare moments for reflection and celebration.

This shift allowed me to spotlight my guests—their stories, expertise, and wisdom became the heart of the show. Despite my introverted nature, I found that creating space for others to share their journeys brought me immense joy and fulfillment.

Starting a podcast doesn't require expensive equipment or complicated software. Here's what I used:

- **An external microphone:** Clear audio is essential for a professional feel.
- **A computer or mobile phone:** Either works perfectly for recording.

- **BeeKonnected:** A free, versatile platform for recording and hosting interviews.
- **Calendly app:** Crucial for scheduling interviews and staying organized.
- **ChatGPT:** A helpful tool for generating and editing guest bios.

Initially, I asked guests to introduce themselves. Later, I refined this approach by preparing their introductions in advance, emphasizing their expertise and creating a warm, professional tone for the show.

Everything about *Inspired Choice Today* was guided by intuition. From selecting guests to choosing topics, I trusted my inner voice to lead me. Speaking from the heart became my focus, silencing doubts and fears that had once held me back.

The lesson here is simple: don't wait for perfection. Take the first step, no matter how small. Speak as if no one is listening, or better yet, talk as if you're sharing your thoughts with yourself. This will attract an audience that resonates with your journey—people who are just a step or two behind you and eager to learn from your experiences.

Setting the stage for my podcast wasn't just about equipment or logistics—it was about courage, commitment, and faith. If you have a dream, don't hesitate. Start where you are, use what you have, and trust the process. Every great journey begins with a single step.

And so, the stage was set. The microphone was on, the guests were ready, and my dream was finally becoming reality.

3. THE POWER OF PERSISTENCE

One of my favorite chapters in *Think and Grow Rich* by Napoleon Hill is the one on persistence. Persistence, as Hill explains, is the cornerstone of success. Without it, we give up too early—before the fruits of our labor have had a chance to blossom. For me, persistence has been the driving force behind *Inspired Choice Today*.

Starting a podcast was a leap of faith, but staying consistent was the real challenge. Like any new endeavor, there were moments when I hit plateaus and had to push myself to the next level. Each shift required stepping outside my comfort zone and into the unknown. It was a constant process of learning, adapting, and growing.

Every new step began with courage. Whether it was reaching out to potential guests or mastering the technical side of podcasting, persistence kept me going. I quickly learned that challenges are inevitable, especially when you're breaking new ground.

For example, I faced practical obstacles, like running out of storage on my laptop. The solution? Cloud storage. I also had to overcome the fear of rejection. Inviting guests—especially high-profile ones—was daunting at first. But I reframed rejection as "not yet." I followed up politely, often getting a "yes" after a few tries.

Flexibility became another key lesson. Sometimes technology failed, requiring last-minute changes to meeting links or platforms. Guests rescheduled, and I had to adjust. Each challenge became an opportunity to adapt, grow, and persist.

Persistence is about more than just not giving up—it's about consistency. I committed to recording episodes regularly. Early on, I opened my calendar for up to 12 hours a day, five days a week, to accommodate guests. As the podcast grew, I refined my schedule to four days a week with shorter windows and now to two days with VIP option for weekends.

The first year of podcasting was a boot camp in persistence. I learned to:

1. **Handle setbacks with flexibility:** Technology glitches and scheduling changes taught me to stay calm and pivot.

2. **Value authentic conversations:** I avoided pre-interviews, allowing my guests' stories to unfold naturally during recording. This made the conversations genuine and impactful.

3. **Turn dreams into action:** I overcame the "knowing-doing gap" by taking small, consistent steps every day.

Through it all, I stayed committed to my vision. Even when I felt self-doubt, I reminded myself: "If I want to be free, I have to be me." That authenticity became the heart of my podcast.

Persistence doesn't just apply to podcasting. It's the secret to achieving any goal. Start small. Take the first step in faith, and let the journey unfold. You're not alone—there's a world of opportunities and people ready to collaborate with you.

Your dreams are worth the effort. Stay consistent. Be flexible. And above all, have fun. That's the power of persistence.

4. THE INSPIRED RECORDS: HIGHLIGHT EPISODES

Every journey has defining moments, and my podcasting journey has been no exception. Along the way, certain episodes stood out as milestones—conversations that left a lasting impression on me and, I hope, on you too. These episodes capture the essence of what *Inspired Choice Today* is all about: connecting with incredible individuals, sharing transformative insights, and embracing the beauty of growth and learning.

From the excitement of hosting my very first guest in **Episode 4**, to the joy of finding my rhythm in **Episode 88**, and finally, to the profound impact of a life-changing conversation in **Episode 365**, each of these highlights represents a pivotal moment in this journey.

These episodes are more than just recordings; they are reflections of persistence, growth, and the power of meaningful dialogue. Let me take you behind the scenes to explore the stories, lessons, and inspiration these standout moments have brought into my life—and, hopefully, yours as well.

To listen to inspiring conversations, check out The Inspired Choice Today podcast on Spotify, Apple Podcasts, Deezer, Audible, Amazon Music, and other streaming platforms. You can also watch interviews on YouTube.

For the easiest access, visit the podcast website at https://www.podcast.inspiredchoice.today/ and search for the guest's name. Don't miss the highlight: an AI-powered chat where you can ask questions about the guests and their expertise! Have fun with this!

4.1 Amazing Soul – My very first Guest

Every journey begins with a single step, and for me, the fourth episode of *Inspired Choice Today* was exactly that—a leap into the unknown. I had the pleasure of welcoming my very first guest, someone I had never spoken to before, known as Amazing Soul. Her name alone intrigued me, and the connection we formed during this interview left an indelible mark on my journey as a podcast host.

This was my introduction to the art of embracing the unknown, trusting my intuition, and creating space for meaningful dialogue. Amazing Soul brought an energy that was both grounding and inspiring. She radiated authenticity, and her philosophy of life—that it should be fun and uncomplicated—was infectious.

One of the most profound moments in our conversation was when Amazing Soul emphasized the importance of being in the now. "To be here now, to be present, to navigate this mishap from moment to moment—that's what inspires me every day," she shared. These words resonated deeply with me, reminding me to ground myself in the present and to give my full attention to the person I'm with.

This wasn't just advice; it was a way of life. She described how her partner serves as a mirror, inspiring her to stay rooted in the moment. It became clear that presence is not only a gift to ourselves but also to those around us.

When I asked how she inspires others, her response was simple yet powerful: by being her authentic self, unapologetically. "I choose to love every part of me regardless," she said, "and just show up as I am." This authenticity was her gift to the world, a message of self-acceptance and empowerment that resonated with me and, I'm sure, with our listeners.

Her philosophy of embracing the unknown and trusting that life will unfold as it's meant to was a revelation. It's a reminder that we don't need elaborate strategies to navigate life—we just need to trust ourselves and take it one step at a time.

Another highlight was her emphasis on the power of breath. "Just breathe," she said, describing it as a simple yet transformative tool to center oneself. Often overlooked, the act of intentional breathing is a reminder of life's simplicity and the resources we already have within us.

She likened this to the fish in water, unable to see the very thing it's surrounded by. The analogy struck a chord—how often do we take for granted the tools and gifts already within our reach?

Reflections on the First Interview

Hosting my first guest was a milestone, but it also came with its challenges. I had never spoken to her before, and this was the first time we connected outside of text. There was uncertainty, yet there was also magic in the unknown. Amazing Soul taught me to embrace the unknown with curiosity and openness.

This episode became a mirror for me as much as it was for her. It reflected my own ability to step into the moment and trust the process. It showed me the beauty of authentic conversation—unrehearsed, unscripted, and deeply human.

Looking back, I realized how much I learned from this single conversation. I learned to trust my intuition, to let go of the need for control, and to celebrate the simple joys of connection and presence. These lessons continue to guide me, not only in podcasting but in life.

Why This Episode Matters

This episode set the tone for everything that followed. It wasn't just an interview—it was a moment of alignment, a testament to the power of inspired choices. Amazing Soul reminded me, and I hope all of you, that the present moment is all we have. "This is it," she said. "There's no moment coming. The magic starts to unfold when you understand that this is it."

Her message of simplicity, authenticity, and presence is one I carry with me to this day. It's a reminder that every moment, every connection, is an opportunity to inspire and be inspired.

I will forever be grateful for this conversation and the wisdom it brought into my life. Amazing Soul truly lives up to her name, and her presence on my podcast marked the beginning of a journey I will always cherish.

As she says, "Be here now." Let this be a call to action for all of us. Take a deep breath, embrace the unknown, and trust that the magic of life will unfold exactly as it's meant to.

Season 1, Episode 4, aired 12/13/2023
recorded 12/13/23, Fayetteville, NC, US / San Diego, CA, US

Connect with Amazing Soul: http://www.themindfckco.com/
The Truth is: I do not know: https://amzn.to/3CYtdaU

4.2 Troy R Chadwick – Patience and Persistence

In *Inspired Choice Today*'s 88 episode, I had the privilege of speaking with Troy R Chadwick, a co-founder of Elevitality and a passionate advocate for personal growth and transformation. What made this interview stand out wasn't just Troy's wisdom and insights, but the palpable energy he brought into the conversation. His deep understanding of the principles of thought, persistence, and purpose created a captivating dialogue that I was honored to share with our audience.

When I asked Troy what inspires him to get up early every day, his answer was beautifully simple: *vision*. Without a clear vision, as he explained, people lack direction and momentum. For Troy, having a goal to strive toward provides the motivation to not only get out of bed but to approach the day with energy and purpose. This insight was a powerful reminder that clarity in our aspirations is the fuel for progress.

Troy's perspective on vision aligned perfectly with one of my favorite quotes: "Without vision, people perish." His advice to lock into what excites you and allows you to grow resonated deeply. It reminded me of the importance of staying connected to our dreams and using them as anchors to navigate life's challenges.

One of the most enlightening parts of the interview was Troy's explanation of thought as a creative force. Drawing inspiration from George Lucas and the conceptualization of *The Force* in *Star Wars*, Troy explored how thoughts are energy, magnets that attract and shape our reality. This idea—that our thoughts are the starting point for everything we experience—offered a fresh perspective on how we approach our goals and challenges.

Troy's passion for sharing these concepts was infectious. He even introduced us to a book that influenced George Lucas, *The Land of the Gods* by H.P. Blavatsky. As he explained, the essence of the *Star Wars* universe is rooted in the metaphysical principles of thought and vibration—a fascinating revelation that tied together storytelling, spirituality, and personal development.

Troy's philosophy on making people smile was elegantly simple: *Smile first.* "Like attracts like," he said, explaining that a genuine smile can spark joy and connection, provided the other person is open to receiving it. This small but meaningful act of positivity is a reflection of how Troy inspires others—by embodying the change he wishes to see in the world.

The most profound takeaway from this conversation was Troy's emphasis on persistence. He highlighted how staying committed to a goal—even in the face of setbacks and challenges—is essential for success. "Stick to the goal, not the plan," he advised, acknowledging that while paths may change, the destination remains constant.

Persistence, paired with patience, was a recurring theme in our discussion. Troy shared how these qualities have guided him through his journey with Elevitality and his broader mission of helping others transform their lives. His message was clear: progress comes not from knowing but from doing. Repetition and consistent application are the keys to embedding new habits and creating lasting change.

As we spoke, it became evident that Troy doesn't just talk about personal growth—he lives it. His ability to simplify complex ideas into actionable insights is a testament to his gift as a leader. Whether discussing the creative power of thought, the importance of vision, or the principles of persistence, Troy's words were filled with a sense of purpose and authenticity.

One of the most memorable moments was when Troy emphasized the importance of being an example. "You cannot inspire someone else unless you are inspired yourself," he said. This perspective reminded me of the ripple effect of personal transformation—how our growth can inspire and elevate those around us.

Troy's closing words were particularly meaningful to me. He acknowledged my persistence in creating and growing *Inspired Choice Today*, celebrating it as a testament to the principles we discussed. This episode wasn't just an interview—it was a step toward my own vision, a manifestation of the goals I've set for myself and the mission I'm committed to.

As Troy said, "You have within you everything you need to make the changes in your life." This message is one I hope resonates with every listener of this episode. It's a reminder that we are all capable of achieving our dreams, provided we stay persistent, patient, and open to growth.

This conversation with Troy R Chadwick left me inspired and energized to continue my journey. It reaffirmed the importance of vision, thought, and persistence—not just as abstract concepts but as practical tools for creating the life we desire.

Thank you, Troy, for sharing your wisdom and being a part of this journey. And to all my listeners, remember: the key to success lies in action. Dream big, think clearly, and persist—always.

Season 2, Episode 44, aired 2/6/2024
recorded 2/4/2024 , La Palma, CA, US / Bavaria, Germany
Connect with Troy R Chadwick: http://www.elevitality.com/

4.3 Brian Proctor – In His Father's Image

In reflecting on my interview with Brian Proctor for episode 96 of Inspired Choice Today, I was struck by the profound simplicity of his message: to live as the best version of yourself, every day. Our conversation was deeply personal, weaving together insights from his book, *My Father Knew the Secret: Growing Up with Bob Proctor,* and his reflections on the extraordinary bond he shared with his father, the legendary Bob Proctor. It was a conversation full of warmth, wisdom, and actionable advice for anyone seeking to live a more fulfilling life.

Brian's mission, as he described it, is to carry forward his father's legacy while offering his unique perspective. His book is not just about Bob Proctor, the motivational speaker seen on stages or in *The Secret*; it's a heartfelt look at Bob as a father, a friend, and a man who lived his principles daily. One story that stood out to me was Brian's memory of early morning phone calls with his father, where they would engage in a practice that was as profound as it was simple—speaking good about others behind their backs. This daily habit of focusing on the positive not only strengthened their connection but also elevated their outlook on life. It's a practice that speaks volumes about the kind of person Bob Proctor was and the lessons he imparted to those closest to him.

Throughout our conversation, Brian emphasized the importance of having a goal, a vision that inspires you to take action every day. For him, carrying forward his father's teachings and helping others realize their potential has become that driving force. It was humbling to hear how he navigates his own journey, building on his father's principles while embracing his unique approach. As Brian put it, none of us need to imitate anyone else; our task is to shine our own light and bring our authentic selves into the world.

What truly resonated with me was Brian's perspective on relationships. He shared how his father's unwavering support made a profound impact on his life, and he now strives to be that cheerleader for others, especially his own children. He reminded me—and, I hope, all listeners—of the power of encouragement and the importance of creating a safe space where others feel empowered to pursue their dreams. Brian's advice to only share your deepest desires with those you trust to support you is a nugget of wisdom that I know will stay with me for a long time.

Our discussion also touched on overcoming discomfort and stepping into the unknown, a lesson Brian himself has embraced since releasing his book. He admitted that stepping into the podcasting world and sharing his story has been a stretch beyond his comfort zone, but one that has brought him immense joy and growth. His words were a powerful reminder that every step we take toward our goals—no matter how small—compounds over time and leads to remarkable transformation.

Brian's message to "be the best version of yourself every day" is both inspiring and attainable. It doesn't demand perfection or grand gestures; it simply asks us to strive for incremental improvement, even in the face of adversity. By focusing on what we can control and showing up as our best selves, we not only improve our own lives but also create a ripple effect of positivity and possibility for those around us.

As I wrapped up our conversation, I couldn't help but feel deeply grateful for the wisdom Brian shared and the reminder of how impactful simple, intentional actions can be. This episode left me inspired to reflect on my own journey and how I can continue to show up, both for myself and for others. To those who read this, I hope you find the same spark of inspiration to take even one small step today toward becoming the best version of yourself. That, as Brian beautifully articulated, is where the magic begins.

Season 3, Episode 8, aired 2/14/2024
recorded 1/29/24 Toronto, Canada / Bavaria, Germany

Connect with Brian Proctor: https://brianproctor.com/
My Father Knew the Secret: https://amzn.to/4iakqma

4.4 Shawnti Refuge – The Power of Journaling

Shawnti Refuge's story is a journey of healing, transformation, and empowerment that resonates deeply. As I sat down with her for this conversation, her authenticity and grounded energy immediately drew me in. Shawnti's work as a certified mental health coach, advocate, keynote speaker, and author is a reflection of her personal experiences and her commitment to helping others navigate their mental and emotional health. Her mission is simple yet profound: to guide women in releasing pain, healing, and living their best lives, all through the transformative power of guided journaling.

When I asked Shawnti what inspires her to rise each day, her response was beautifully selfless. "Someone out there needs my help," she said with conviction. For Shawnti, her work is not about her—it's about service. This sense of purpose fuels her daily, and it's a testament to the depth of her dedication to uplifting others.

As our conversation unfolded, Shawnti shared her thoughts on launching her own podcast. While she doesn't have one yet, the idea is clearly on her radar. When asked who she would invite as a guest, she offered a powerful answer: anyone with a story of overcoming emotional or mental challenges. Shawnti believes in the importance of creating a community where people can see that they are not alone. Her mission is to provide a platform where personal stories inspire others to find hope and healing. She also shared her perspective on celebrities, emphasizing her focus on authenticity over fame.

Her openness about her own struggles is central to how she inspires others. Diagnosed with severe anxiety and depression in 2018, Shawnti speaks candidly about her journey. She describes the raw and painful moments with honesty, letting people see where she's been and how far she's come. "I came from this," she says, "and look at me now." Her transparency and willingness to share her story offer hope to those who are struggling, reminding them that healing and transformation are possible.

Shawnti's clients and community are drawn to her honesty and grounded nature. She describes herself as an open book, unafraid to speak the truth even when it's difficult. "I'm very blunt," she admits, "but I don't use my honesty to hurt anyone intentionally." This straightforward approach sets her apart as a coach and advocate. She is committed to holding her clients accountable while teaching them how to face their triggers and heal holistically.

Shawnti's turning point came in 2018 when she felt an overwhelming cloud of darkness over her. This led her to seek help, beginning with her family doctor and eventually finding a therapist who introduced her to the power of journaling. Initially resistant to the idea, Shawnti soon discovered how transformative journaling could be. This practice not only helped her heal but also inspired her to create her own line of guided journals. Each journal is tailored to specific topics, offering prompts, affirmations, and space for reflection. Today, she has published 26 guided journals and uses them as a cornerstone of her work with clients.

As our conversation neared its end, I asked Shawnti about the one benefit people gain when they connect with her. Her answer was simple yet profound: "I speak life into people." Shawnti's goal is to ensure that everyone who interacts with her leaves feeling better than when they arrived. Whether through a casual conversation, a coaching session, or a recommendation for a journal, Shawnti pours her energy and compassion into uplifting others.

Her guiding principle is to be the person she needed during her darkest times. This mission drives her work and resonates in every aspect of her approach. Shawnti's journey is a testament to the power of facing pain, embracing healing, and using personal experiences to help others. Her story is one of resilience, authenticity, and an unwavering commitment to making a difference.

Season 3, Episode 22, aired 2/28/2024
recorded 2/8/2024 Fresno, TX, US / Bavaria, Germany

Connect with Shawnti: https://shawntirefugejournals.com/
Quiet As Kept: https://amzn.to/3OA3Ajd

4.5 Jeffrey Gitomer – The King of Sales

Episode 111 of *Inspired Choice Today* was a vibrant and insightful conversation with the legendary Jeffrey Gitomer, often hailed as "The King of Sales." Jeffrey's energy and wisdom flowed seamlessly, offering a wealth of practical insights that felt both accessible and transformative. From his journey as a prolific author of 17 books to his approach to inspiring others, Jeffrey shared lessons rooted in authenticity, connection, and the power of belief.

What stood out immediately was Jeffrey's emphasis on self-inspiration. He eloquently explained that inspiring oneself first is the foundation for inspiring others. This perspective resonated deeply, as it underscores the importance of personal alignment before attempting to influence the world around us. Jeffrey's ability to infuse his work with passion and genuine care for others was palpable throughout our discussion.

We delved into his iconic books, like *The Little Red Book of Selling*, which has become a touchstone for sales professionals worldwide. Jeffrey's philosophy on writing, which began with weekly columns that organically evolved into his first book, is a testament to the power of consistent action. His story serves as a reminder that big projects often emerge naturally when approached with steady commitment and love for the process.

Jeffrey's insights into the sales process were equally compelling. He emphasized the importance of building trust and understanding others through thoughtful questions. For Jeffrey, sales isn't just about transactions; it's about forming genuine connections. He reminded us that people buy from those they trust and enjoy being around, a truth that transcends industries and cultures.

One of the most striking elements of our conversation was Jeffrey's "reading room," a sacred space filled with books and artifacts that inspire him daily. This 3x3-meter room, devoid of windows but brimming with energy, is where he draws his creative strength. His dedication to immersing himself in an environment of inspiration speaks to the importance of cultivating spaces that fuel our passions.

Jeffrey also shared his belief in adapting inspiration to the culture and environment around you. Drawing from his experiences in Berlin, he noted how cultural nuances shape how people perceive and respond to humor, trust, and interaction. This lesson, to adapt inspiration to context, is a valuable takeaway for anyone working across diverse settings.

When discussing his approach to sales training, Jeffrey highlighted the significance of learning through real-world experiences. While books and courses can provide foundational knowledge, true mastery comes from observing, practicing, and refining in the field. His advice to new salespeople to align their work with their passions felt particularly impactful: "Find something you love and do that. Speak from your heart, not just your head."

As our conversation wound down, Jeffrey left us with a poignant reminder: "If you want to build wealth, first build a wealth of knowledge." His belief in the transformative power of daily study and personal growth echoed throughout the episode. He also touched on the role of belief—not just in oneself, but in the products and companies one represents—as a cornerstone of success.

Jeffrey's authenticity, humor, and generosity made this interview a true delight. His openness to connecting with listeners—whether through his email, website, or upcoming initiatives—reflects his commitment to helping others succeed. For those seeking inspiration, actionable advice, or simply a boost of energy, Jeffrey Gitomer's words are a beacon. As he aptly put it, "Study every day, and you'll get better every day."

As I reflect on this interview, I feel grateful for the insights Jeffrey shared and the opportunity to learn from someone who embodies his message so fully. His parting wisdom, to "build a wealth of knowledge," was not only inspiring but also a challenge I'm eager to embrace. It's a reminder to keep growing, keep learning, and keep sharing—not just for myself but for the community I'm so passionate about serving.

Season 3, Episode 23, aired 2/29/2024
recorded 2/21/24, Charlotte, NC, US / Bavaria, Germany

Connect with Jeffrey Gitomer: https://www.gitomer.com/
Little Red Book of Selling: https://amzn.to/4fUJ9ti

4.6 Nellie Harden – The 6570 Family Project

As I sat down to talk with Nellie Harden, I was instantly struck by her warmth and clarity of purpose. A family leadership coach with a focus on building worth, esteem, and confidence in young women before they leave home, Nellie brings a refreshingly authentic approach to a subject that often feels elusive. Her mission, however, extends beyond raising the next generation; she also helps adult women navigate their own journeys of self-worth and rediscovery.

Nellie began by sharing her own story, which is one of transformation born from both personal struggles and an unshakable determination. She described the "6,570 days" — the total number of days in 18 years — as the critical period for building the foundation of worth that can sustain a person throughout life. As a young woman, she admitted to chasing external validation in the absence of a solid internal foundation, something many of us can relate to. Awards, grades, work, and relationships became placeholders for worth, but each came with sharp edges that left her with dramas and traumas to unpack later in life.

This realization came into sharp focus when she became a mother to four daughters. In a particularly poignant moment, Nellie found herself in a hospital room with a newborn, two toddlers, and a four-year-old while her husband was gravely ill. Looking at her daughters, she knew she had to act fast to give them the tools she herself lacked. "Now is the time," she told herself. "I have a very limited amount of time to build these foundations in you."

Nellie shifted careers, moving from working with animals in marine biology to the decidedly messier world of humans. Since

2010, she has been helping families establish what she calls "inside-out worth," a process that teaches young women to see their value and trust themselves, rather than relying on external validation. Her insights are grounded in both her professional background and her deeply personal experiences.

When I asked Nellie what inspires her, her answer was simple yet profound: her daughters. Watching them navigate the world and seeing the challenges young women face today drives her every day. She spoke about the importance of equipping young women to wake up each day with a sense of purpose, asking, "How can I serve the world today?" rather than waiting for the world to define them. It's a message of empowerment and accountability, and one she's committed to spreading far and wide.

Nellie credits her faith and the Bible as her first and foremost source of guidance, but she also highlighted the influence of Brené Brown, with whom she worked for 18 months. Brené's work on vulnerability gave Nellie the tools to face her own traumas and helped her reframe vulnerability as a strength rather than a weakness. "Vulnerability is a key tool of self-disciplined leadership," she explained, adding that we all need to lead ourselves, even if we never lead anyone else.

Our conversation took an insightful turn when Nellie talked about the balance between feelings and behavior. "Feelings can't be in the driver's seat," she explained, noting that critical thinking must come between feelings and actions. This nuanced approach allows her to help clients navigate the often-messy terrain of emotions while still holding themselves accountable for their actions.

Nellie's ability to connect deeply with others is one of her greatest gifts, a trait she attributes to her mother. Growing up, she watched her mom strike up conversations with anyone and everyone, and that ability to relate to others' stories became a cornerstone of Nellie's own work. "When you strip everything away, we all share the same human emotions—joy, love, shame, guilt, happiness," she said. "That's what makes us relatable."

Looking ahead to 2024, Nellie revealed an exciting goal: writing her first solo book. After co-authoring projects and publishing journals, she's ready to put her unique approach to leadership and worth-building into a format that can reach even more people. It's clear that she's driven by a desire to help others see the potential within themselves and to create their own personalized paths to success.

Before we wrapped up, Nellie shared her guiding mantra: "Discipline yourself so others don't have to." It's a reminder that self-leadership and accountability are the keys to unlocking a life of purpose and fulfillment. For anyone raising or leading young women—or looking to rediscover their own worth—Nellie Harden's work is a beacon of hope and transformation.

As we said our goodbyes, I felt deeply inspired by Nellie's journey, her mission, and her unwavering commitment to helping others. If you'd like to explore her resources or connect with her, visit her website at nellieharden.com, where you can find masterclasses, downloads, and updates on her upcoming book. Nellie's passion is contagious, and her message is one we all need to hear.

Season 6, Episode 40, aired 7/29/2024
recorded 6/20/24, Southport, NC, US / Bavaria, Germany

Connect with Nellie: https://www.nellieharden.com/resources

4.7 Suzanne Butler – The Energy of Feng Shui

As I sat down to speak with Suzanne Butler for this episode of *Inspired Choice Today*, I was immediately captivated by her warm presence and profound understanding of Feng Shui. Suzanne is a practitioner who helps people create balance and joy in their lives by harnessing the energies of their homes. Her unique approach has brought transformation to countless lives, and I was eager to dive deeper into her world.

Suzanne began by explaining how Feng Shui works. While the concept might seem complex at first, she has mastered its intricacies to the point where it feels almost magical. "Basically, I harness the energies in your home to either improve what's going on or reduce the bad things," Suzanne shared. From improving relationships to resolving financial difficulties, her work identifies and neutralizes negative energies while amplifying positive ones. What struck me most was her statement: "You don't even need to believe in it for it to work."

Suzanne detailed how her process doesn't necessarily involve rearranging furniture. Instead, it's about understanding the unique energy map of each home. Every house, she explained, is influenced by factors like its orientation, construction date, and even renovations. This makes every home's energy needs distinct, even if it looks identical to its neighbors from the outside. "Each area of your home represents an area of your life," Suzanne explained. Using remedies, she works with the home's energy to address the specific needs of its occupants, often achieving dramatic results.

One of the most fascinating aspects Suzanne touched on was how energies shift over time. She shared a story about a client who had suffered significant health and mental challenges since the start of the year. After an assessment, Suzanne discovered that the energies of the client's home had shifted into a negative cycle, amplifying existing issues. By implementing remedies, Suzanne was able to help her client restore balance. It's this type of transformation, Suzanne said, that inspires her to continue her work.

Her path to becoming a Feng Shui practitioner was born out of necessity. Ten years ago, Suzanne was struggling with illness, a toxic relationship, and financial instability. Despite her efforts to fix these issues through traditional means, nothing seemed to work. Feng Shui became her last resort—and within days of applying its principles, her life began to shift. Money flowed, her toxic relationship ended, and opportunities opened up. "Once you implement it properly and make a concerted effort, you can experience change within hours, even days," she said.

Suzanne's clients, in turn, inspire her. She shared stories of individuals who've left toxic relationships, achieved financial windfalls, and found new strength to tackle life's challenges. Her approach is straightforward yet compassionate. "I don't sugarcoat anything," she said. "I tell it as it is, but always with kindness." Her honesty and deep intuition have made her a trusted guide for many.

During our conversation, Suzanne emphasized the ripple effect of balanced homes. "If everyone had a home that supported their greater good, imagine the impact," she said. This vision drives her goal of helping 100 women in 2024 create balanced homes, indirectly supporting 400 people in living more joyful, abundant lives. Suzanne believes this work is particularly important for women, who often put others first. "When women thrive, everyone around them benefits," she said.

For Suzanne, the power of Feng Shui goes beyond personal transformation—it's about creating a collective shift toward positivity and healing. As she said, "If we don't heal, we don't move forward. It's as simple as that."

Suzanne's closing message was a powerful reminder: "You deserve better than good. Your life might be good, but why not aim for great? Feng Shui can give that to you."

If you'd like to explore Suzanne's work, visit her website for free resources, including a manifestation challenge, a home energy quiz, and masterclasses. As I reflected on our conversation, I couldn't help but feel inspired by Suzanne's passion and dedication to making the world a better place, one home at a time.

Season 5, Episode 38, aired 6/10/2024
recorded 5/6/2024 Brisbane, Australia / Bavaria, Germany

Connect with Suzanne: https://harmonisingenergies.com.au/

4.8 Adedayo Adeniji – Poetry of Purpose

Sitting down with Dayo Adeniji was like stepping into a sanctuary of wisdom and faith. Dayo, a spiritual poet with a heart for meaningful connection, has a remarkable ability to transform profound truths into inspiring verses. Her poetry resonates deeply, leaving readers feeling enlightened and captivated. Beginning her poetic journey as a teenager, Dayo has shaped her unique voice through life's experiences, the Bible's wisdom, and an unyielding commitment to inspire others.

When asked what inspires her daily, Dayo's response was grounded in gratitude and observation. "I'm inspired by creation," she shared. "The intricate design of our world, the resilience of people overcoming challenges, and my faith in God fill me with awe. Reading the Bible never fails to ignite my creativity—it's not my wisdom, but God's, that I channel into my poetry and songs."

Dayo's spiritual poetry is not merely art; it's a message. Her work is a testament to overcoming barriers, as she revealed her earlier struggles with shyness and introversion. Through her faith community, she gained confidence by participating in worship teams and charitable work. It was within this supportive environment that she began performing her poems and songs. "God's spirit gave me strength to share my voice," she said, "and now I'm ready to bring my message beyond those walls."

Throughout our conversation, Dayo frequently highlighted the importance of transformation and perseverance. Her admiration for figures like Nelson Mandela and Mother Teresa reflects her appreciation for those who turn hardships into acts of love and service. "People who choose not to take revenge, but instead bring peace and healing, inspire me deeply," she said. It's this mindset that fuels her creative process.

One particularly moving moment in our interview came when Dayo discussed the power of channeling personal experiences into her poetry. "I've moved a lot in my life," she explained. "Meeting diverse people taught me that everyone's story is unique. Their struggles inspired my book, *Deja Vu, God Loves You, Not Impossible*. It's for those who feel like giving up. Through poetry, I want them to see that their weaknesses can become strengths."

Dayo's book title encapsulates her mission: to show that faith, hope, and love are transformative forces. She continues to explore creative ways to share her message, such as repurposing her poetry for social media and engaging in workshops. "I'm learning to market my books," she admitted with a smile, "because the words need to reach those who need them most."

In addition to writing, Dayo's goals include conquering imposter syndrome and launching a faith-centered business. "People need faith, hope, and love, especially in today's changing world," she said. With her characteristic humility, Dayo shared how John 3:16 guides her work: "For God so loved the world that He gave His one and only Son... that's the heart of everything I write."

For Dayo, poetry is not merely a creative outlet but a divine calling. Her unique gift lies in translating spiritual insights into accessible, thought-provoking verses. "I ask God questions, and through prayer and reflection, the answers come as poetry," she explained. Her work offers a fresh perspective on the timeless connection between faith and creativity.

In her closing message to our audience, Dayo left us with heartfelt encouragement: "Don't give up. Build strong relationships, love deeply, and never stop praying. God loves you so much." These words perfectly encapsulate her mission: to uplift, inspire, and remind us of the boundless love and hope that faith brings.

Dayo's journey is a testament to the transformative power of faith, resilience, and creative expression. Her ability to translate life's complexities into impactful poetry makes her a beacon of inspiration. To explore her work further, including her book *Deja Vu, God Loves You, Not Impossible*, visit her work website and connect. Never stop chasing your dreams—Dayo's poetry is here to remind you that, with faith, nothing is impossible.

Season 8, Episode 8, aired 9/22/24
recorded Wembley, United Kingdom / Bavaria, Germany

Connect with Dayo: https://adedayoadeniji.com/
Get the book: Déjà Vu, God Loves You: Not Impossible:
https://amzn.to/3ZaS3vm

4.9 Shane Perry – From Comfort to Success

Shane Perry's story is one of transformation, resilience, and an unwavering commitment to helping others unlock their potential. Sitting down with Shane was a deeply insightful experience as he shared his journey from a successful entrepreneur to a dedicated performance consultant. Shane's ability to guide individuals from comfort to achievement is grounded in decades of experience and personal breakthroughs. After facing the tragic loss of his 19-year-old daughter, Shane found renewed purpose in his mission to help people break free from mediocrity and achieve high-performance lives.

Shane began by recounting his career, which spans 35 years of building and leading teams. He described how his fascination with human behavior and motivation led him to study psychology in depth, ultimately developing a system to empower people to set and achieve their goals. This foundation paved the way for his current work as the founder of *Disruption Factor*. The name is no coincidence—Shane believes that disruption is the catalyst for growth. He's created an online course, *From Comfort Zone to Success*, designed to equip individuals with the tools they need to overcome fear, procrastination, and self-doubt.

One of the key themes of our conversation was the pervasive comfort zone that holds so many back. Shane explained that the comfort zone, shaped by our paradigms, habits, and fears, is the enemy of success. With a deep understanding of how these mental constructs form, Shane helps clients identify the traits that keep them stuck. He openly shared his own struggles with procrastination, fear of rejection, and concern about others' opinions—traits he has worked to overcome. "Your comfort zone is built by your habits and fears," he explained. "But success lies outside of it."

Shane's practical strategies for goal-setting are as inspiring as they are actionable. He emphasized the importance of writing down goals, cultivating a vision, and creating a tangible plan to achieve them. But he didn't shy away from the challenges, noting that disruption—the resistance and discomfort that arise when we try to change—often sends people back to their comfort zones. He calls this the "disruption factor" and teaches his clients how to navigate it. "When you set a goal, you'll face disruption before you see success," Shane said. "Understanding that is key to pushing forward."

When asked about the most rewarding part of his work, Shane spoke passionately about witnessing his clients' transformations. For him, the ultimate reward is helping people build a new comfort zone—one where achieving their goals becomes second nature. He recounted his own fitness journey as an example, sharing how he went from struggling to establish healthy habits to reaching a point where skipping a workout felt uncomfortable. "When you get to that place," he said, "you've won."

As we delved deeper into his approach, Shane underscored the importance of addressing the mental barriers shaped by societal norms and middle-class paradigms. "Most of us are trained to settle," he said. "We're taught to avoid risks and stay safe. But true success requires stepping into the unknown." By helping clients reframe their paradigms and focus on possibilities instead of limitations, Shane equips them to break free from mediocrity and achieve their full potential.

Shane also shared his perspective on the broader applications of his work, including seminars and new ventures for his growing business. His personal goal is to continue his fitness journey, pushing himself to new levels of health and wellness. Professionally, he's focused on expanding *Disruption Factor* through seminars and workshops, turning what started as a passion project into a thriving business.

In his final message, Shane left listeners with a powerful call to action: "Take the plunge. Don't wait for January 1 to change your life. Start now. Whether you see results immediately or not, the fact that you're doing it will feed your soul. In a world full of starters, be a finisher."

Shane Perry's insights are a testament to the power of stepping out of your comfort zone and embracing the challenges that come with growth. His journey is an inspiring reminder that disruption, while uncomfortable, is the gateway to achieving the life you truly desire. For those ready to take the leap, Shane's work offers the guidance and tools needed to navigate the path to success. To learn more, visit his website at *disruption-factor.com* or follow him on Instagram @realshaneperry.

Season 11, Episode 20, aired 2/3/2025
recorded 10/24/24 Arroya Grande, CA, US / Bavaria, Germany

Connect with Shane: https://www.disruption-factor.com/
Crossing the Minefield of Life: https://amzn.to/41zv1Bx

4.10 Laura Watson – The Dance of Leadership

When I sat down with Laura Watson, I was immediately captivated by her grounded energy and laser-sharp clarity. Laura, an award-winning coach, world country dance champion, and someone who has dedicated over 30 years to helping people unlock their full potential, shared insights that felt both profound and refreshingly actionable. Our conversation left me inspired, and I'm confident it will do the same for you.

One of the most striking moments of our interview was Laura's approach to bridging the gap between theory and practice in leadership. "You have to start with clarity," she emphasized. "Clarity about what you want, how you're going to accomplish it, and when." She described how many of her clients start with lofty goals, only to get stuck in the quicksand of overwhelm and procrastination. Her solution? Break big objectives into small, actionable steps and, most importantly, schedule those steps.

Laura's advice to "book an appointment with yourself" was a game-changer for me. It's not just about having goals—it's about committing to them by carving out dedicated time in your calendar. She even supports her clients by sending reminders and tracking progress to ensure accountability. Her no-nonsense yet empathetic approach struck a chord, particularly when she described her role as a mix of cheerleader and occasional "butt-kicker."

Laura's passion for country dancing—where she has already claimed a world championship and is training for her next—plays a pivotal role in her coaching. "Nothing I do in dance comes naturally," she shared. "It's all about pushing beyond my comfort zone, feeling the discomfort, and stepping into it."

Her dance journey mirrors the leadership journey she helps her clients navigate. Laura believes that to guide others effectively, she must also "walk the talk." Stretching her own limits makes her coaching relatable and authentic. "We have to get comfortable with discomfort," she said, a mantra that she embodies both on the dance floor and in the boardroom.

When it comes to leadership challenges, Laura has seen it all—especially the struggles leaders face with delegation. She talked about how leaders often default to doing tasks themselves, which stifles growth. "If they keep doing it all, they'll never have the time or capacity to scale their business," she explained.

Her solution? Clear communication and setting expectations about the level of authority being delegated. "It's not just about asking, 'Do you get it?' It's about asking, 'What do you understand?' and giving people a chance to paraphrase." This subtle shift in questioning can mean the difference between a successfully delegated task and one that falls apart.

Feedback, Laura explained, is often where leaders hit emotional roadblocks—both in giving and receiving it. She believes that receiving feedback requires self-awareness to identify triggers. "If feedback feels like an attack, it's often not about the person delivering it but about a story or limiting belief we're carrying."

Her advice? Develop mental and emotional mastery to stay calm and open to feedback. And remember, feedback is an invitation to consider—not a mandate to implement.

Laura closed the conversation with a powerful message: "Step into your leadership and always be looking to level up." Whether it's personal leadership or guiding a team, she emphasized the importance of continuous growth. Her advice? Start where you are, invest in coaching or mastermind groups, and challenge yourself to reach new levels.

This conversation left me in awe of Laura's ability to simplify complex concepts while inspiring action. Her words are a call to anyone ready to embrace clarity, consistency, and courage in pursuit of their goals.

As Laura reminds us, clarity and consistency are the building blocks of success, whether in leadership, business, or life. Start small, stay consistent, and don't be afraid to schedule that all-important appointment with yourself.

Season 10, Episode 84, aired 1/21/2025
recorded Calgary, Alberta, Canada / Bavaria, Germany

Connect with Laura: https://venturecoaching.ca/

4.11 Brian Hite – Begin Again Blueprint

When Brian Hite, PhD sat across from me for our conversation on *Inspired Choice Today*, it was clear from the start that his story was anything but ordinary. From stuntman to key note speaker, author, and sport/performance/organizational psychologist, his journey is a masterclass in embracing change, leaning into uncertainty, and crafting a life that is both dynamic and deeply fulfilling.

Brian's philosophy is encapsulated in the title of his book, *Begin Again: Utilize the Wisdom of Eastern and Western Ideologies to Achieve Your Full Potential*. "I believe we can always begin again," he shared. This perspective isn't just a clever tagline—it's a way of living that has defined his career and personal growth. For Brian, the present moment is not only the starting point but the only point where real change is possible.

As a stuntman with a career spanning 30 years, over 100 films and TV shows, and a prestigious Screen Actor's Guild award for his work on the TV show *24*, Brian knows what it means to perform under pressure. He described the intense focus required to ensure safety and success on set. "When people get caught up thinking about what was or what might be, they miss what is," he explained. This need for presence continues to shape not only his stunt career but also his approach to coaching and teaching.

After years working solely in the entertainment industry, life presented an additional direction – performance psychology. First, it was completing the education he had set aside in his pursuit of stunts. Then came a decade-long role as a performance psychologist working with the U.S. Army, followed by a return to stunt work, only to pivot yet again by adding to the mix his own speaking/coaching business, Brian Hite Global. Each shift, as he described it, was an opportunity to begin again—a chance to merge his diverse experiences into something greater.

What stood out most in our conversation was Brian's unwavering belief in the value of the journey itself. "It's not about the end result," he said. "It's the experience of growing, developing, and improving along the way." This mindset isn't just theoretical; it's practical advice he gives to his clients, whether they're athletes, military personnel, or executives seeking peak performance. His coaching blends Western science and Eastern philosophy, offering a holistic approach that resonates across cultures and industries.

As a keynote speaker and educator, Brian also touched on the importance of trusting the process. He's quick to acknowledge that not every decision leads to success in the conventional sense, but every experience adds depth to our understanding of ourselves and the world. "Even when things don't work out as planned, they're still working out," he said, a statement that has stayed with me.

Brian's ability to distill his diverse experiences—academic, physical, and philosophical—into actionable insights is what makes him a standout leader. His upcoming projects, including his next book, Flow under Fire: *A Stuntman's Guide to Handling Pressure*, and a series of coaching programs targetting pressure, motivation, and consistent peak performance reflect his commitment to helping others harness their potential.

As our interview concluded, he left the audience with this thought: "Opportunity is always there. You just have to be open to seeing it—and to the idea that even when it doesn't look like what you expected, it's still working out." It's a reminder that resonates deeply, whether you're navigating a career pivot, a personal challenge, or simply trying to embrace the present moment.

Brian Hite's story is a testament to the power of resilience, curiosity, and the willingness to start fresh—again and again. It's a lesson that we can all carry into our own lives, knowing that every moment offers a new chance to begin.

Season 11, Episode 42, aired 2/14/2025
recorded 10/28/2024 Nashville, TN, US / Bavaria, Germany

Connect   with   Brian:
https://beginagainperformancepsychology.com/
Begin Again: https://amzn.to/4fSi2iD

4.12 Katherine K Mullin - Inspired by Growth

In this episode, I had the pleasure of sitting down with Katherine Kim Mullin, a woman whose approach to life, business, and connection is as inspiring as it is transformative. Katherine, who balances her professional name with her approachable persona, introduced herself as someone deeply committed to imagining a world of wealth and connectivity for all. For her, being rich isn't merely about money—it's about having the freedom to live life on your terms.

Katherine's 40-plus years of experience, particularly in commercial real estate and business consulting, provide her with a unique perspective on wealth creation. Her philosophy integrates making money, saving money, and, most importantly, connecting with others to multiply opportunities. As she shared during our conversation, wealth isn't just about profit margins; it's about building meaningful relationships that allow all parties to thrive.

One of the standout moments of our discussion was Katherine's perspective on collaboration. She explained how businesses can create exponential value by teaming up with like-minded organizations. For instance, she recounted the story of a friend who designed electronic wheelchairs and another company that specialized in handrails for accessibility. By collaborating, these businesses could not only expand their offerings but also serve their shared clientele more effectively. This spirit of co-creation is central to Katherine's approach, and it's a lesson many entrepreneurs can benefit from.

When I asked Katherine who inspires her, she spoke passionately about the authors and mentors who have shaped her journey. From Zig Ziglar's teachings on goal setting to

Napoleon Hill's timeless principles in *Think and Grow Rich*, she has drawn wisdom from some of the greatest minds in personal development. Interestingly, she credits the Napoleon Hill Foundation for helping her see the deeper layers of Hill's work after decades of studying his book. This immersion in Hill's philosophy not only enriched her understanding but also spurred her to give back by sharing these principles with underserved communities, such as immigrants in Quebec seeking employment.

Katherine's ability to provide insight rather than simply inspire is one of her defining qualities. As she puts it, "I provide insight, and they become inspired." Her mission is to help others see themselves in a new light, offering guidance while encouraging them to find their unique path. This authenticity and clarity are what make her such a powerful connector and mentor.

Another highlight of our conversation was her emphasis on designing life with intentionality. Katherine shared her "four C's" approach: create, choose, connect, and commit. These principles guide her decisions and actions, enabling her to live with clarity, courage, and confidence. She also revealed her unique take on vision boards—she prefers vision maps, which offer a more dynamic and actionable representation of her goals.

For 2024, Katherine has ambitious targets, including launching a groundbreaking project currently in beta testing. Though she couldn't disclose details due to non-disclosure agreements, her excitement and confidence were palpable. This initiative, which stems from her passion for connectivity and collaboration, promises to be a game-changer.

Our conversation was a masterclass in how to combine heart, strategy, and vision to create a life that is both fulfilling and impactful. Katherine's message is clear: success is not about compromise but about investment—in yourself, your relationships, and your dreams.

As our discussion concluded, I couldn't help but feel grateful for the insight Katherine shared. Her words, "You don't find success when you're trying to change each other," will stay with me as a reminder that authenticity and alignment are the keys to meaningful collaboration.

Season 6, Episode 42, aired 7/31/2024
recorded 6/26/24 Montréal, QC, Canada / Bavaria, Germany

Connect with Katherine: http://www.katherinekimmullin.com/

4.13 Laura Lee Kenny – From Roots to Radiance

In the vibrant flow of life's journey, some people stand out not only because of their accomplishments but for their relentless spirit of generosity and transformation. Laura Lee Kenny is one such person, a dear friend and an inspiration whose life story is a testimony to resilience, faith, and the power of constant reinvention.

When I first met Laura Lee in Ottawa in October 2022 at an event hosted by Peggy McColl, I immediately recognized her as someone who exudes warmth and strength. The pandemic had just loosened its grip, and this was my first event in the coaching industry. To meet someone so magnetic and insightful was a gift. As she shared her journey with me, it became clear that Laura Lee was more than a friend—she was a beacon of possibility.

We met again a year later at an event in Los Angeles at the home of Ramy El-Batrawi. Despite the different settings, one thing remained constant: Laura Lee's boundless enthusiasm for life and her mission to help others achieve their full potential.

Laura Lee's story begins in New Brunswick, Canada, where she grew up as the third of 12 children. Born into modest circumstances, she learned the value of hard work early on. Her upbringing, which she describes as "pioneer-style living," instilled a deep sense of resilience and adaptability that would guide her through life's challenges.

Her professional journey is as multifaceted as her personality. Laura Lee excelled in two primary careers—first as an Executive Manager with a cosmetics company and then as a Certified Financial Planner. While the roles may seem worlds apart, the common thread was her ability to empower others, whether it was through beauty products or financial achievements.

In her cosmetics career, she built a network of 123 representatives, inspiring them to achieve their goals. As a financial planner, she broke barriers in an industry traditionally dominated by men, gaining the trust of clients decades older than her. Her ability to meet people where they were and speak their language—financial or otherwise—set her apart.

After 25 years in financial planning, Laura Lee felt a pull toward a new purpose: help clients with their financial achievements. It wasn't just about helping people manage their money; it was about showing them how to create wealth, particularly through passive income streams like affiliate marketing.

Laura Lee is working on setting up a nonprofit *Be Financially Creative*, which embodies this mission: to teach financial literacy, money mindset and passive income streams.. With a goal of reaching 100 students a year, Laura Lee is dedicated to teaching younger generations the financial skills and mindset they need to succeed. Her work is a blend of philanthropy and practicality, guided by the belief that everyone deserves access to financial education.

One of Laura Lee's unique gifts is her ability to connect people. She has an uncanny knack for remembering details and linking individuals with the resources or opportunities they need. This talent, combined with her natural energy and charisma, has earned her the nickname "Wealth Magnet" among her peers.

Despite her many achievements, Laura Lee remains humble and grounded. She attributes her success to her faith and the values instilled in her by her grandparents. Her life is a testament to the idea that spirituality and wealth can coexist harmoniously.

When asked how she inspires others, Laura Lee emphasizes the importance of opening minds to new possibilities. "It's never too late to make a change," she says. Her own journey—pivoting careers, starting a nonprofit, and embracing new opportunities—serves as proof of this belief.

Her approach is deeply personal, meeting people where they are and helping them envision a better future. Whether she's teaching financial literacy, mentoring entrepreneurs, or sharing her story, Laura Lee's goal is to empower others to take control of their lives.

In addition to her nonprofit work, Laura Lee is involved in several ventures that align with her mission of helping others. She is a founding member of another business, where she helps small businesses increase their net profit by 1% daily. She also hosts a podcast, *Money Mindset Mentors*, and offers programs through platforms like *BeeKonnected*.

Laura Lee Kenny's story is one of triumph, faith, and the relentless pursuit of a better world. She has not only transformed her own life but continues to inspire others to do the same. As our conversation ended, I couldn't help but feel grateful for the connection we share and the lessons she continues to teach me.

Season 1, Episode 27, aired 12/19/2023
recorded 12/19/23 New Brunswick, Canada / Echo Park, CA, US

Connect with Laura Lee:
https://www.linkedin.com/in/lauraleekenny/

4.14 Martina Wagner – The Scent of Success

When I sat down with Martina Wagner for our episode of *Inspired Choice Today*, I knew we were about to dive into something extraordinary. Martina isn't just an Elite Success Coach—she's a beacon of calm and inspiration. Her energy radiates a sense of effortless empowerment that has transformed not only her life but also the lives of countless others. She's someone I hold close as a friend, mentor, and collaborator, and I'm honored to share her story with you.

We first met at the Napoleon Hill Institute in early 2023, where we immersed ourselves in the timeless principles of success. That journey expanded into something even more fascinating when Martina introduced me to the world of essential aroma oils. What started as curiosity turned into a revelation. With names like *Abundance* and *Higher Unity*, these oils became more than just scents—they became tools for transformation.

For Martina, these oils aren't just products; they're partners in the coaching journey. She shared how incorporating aromatherapy into her practice helped her sevenfold her income in just 10 months. "It's not just about the oils," she explained, "but about what they represent—belief, abundance, and the limitless possibilities within us all."

Martina's unique approach combines coaching with the subtle yet powerful effects of aromatherapy. Her method is grounded in a belief that everyone holds the potential for greatness within them, waiting to be unlocked. "You need to find your 'why,'" she told me. "That big, burning desire that pushes you forward. And then, with a little Abundance, a little

Believe, and maybe a touch of Higher Unity, you'll watch opportunities rush toward you."

I shared my own journey with her recommended oil, *Higher Unity*, and how I struggled with its scent at first. Her advice? Apply it to the soles of my feet for 10 days—and wear socks if necessary to block the smell. By the end of the experiment, the scent transformed into one of my favorites. This small yet profound shift reminded me of how the simplest actions, done consistently, can lead to significant breakthroughs.

Martina's wisdom doesn't stop at oils. She is deeply inspired by nature, a constant source of abundance and serenity. "Look around," she said. "Mother Nature is filled with unconditional love, growth, and endless possibilities. When we align with that energy and embrace our inner child, we tap into a playful, effortless way of living." Her words painted vivid pictures of palm trees, oceans, and the rolling winds through Austrian forests, reminding us that inspiration is always within reach, no matter where we are.

What sets Martina apart is her ability to reflect the best version of her clients back to them. She believes in the power of energy and vibration, saying, "Words are secondary. It's the frequency you send out that truly inspires others." Her approach is not about fixing people but about helping them rediscover their innate brilliance and step into their higher selves.

As our conversation drew to a close, Martina generously shared a gift for the *Inspired Choice Today* community—a free three-day master class designed to help participants make 2024 their best year yet. From imagination and belief to creating actionable plans, the master class promises to deliver tools for leveling up big time. "You can replay it until Christmas," she said with a smile, knowing that each watch would uncover deeper layers of value.

Martina also extended a special offer for those interested in working with her aroma oils, with nearly 50% off the starting package. It's a testament to her belief in the transformative power of these tools and her desire to share them with as many people as possible.

As we wrapped up, I couldn't help but reflect on how much Martina's friendship and mentorship have enriched my life. Her ability to combine practical strategies with the ethereal beauty of nature and energy work is a gift to all who cross her path. If you're ready to step into your higher self, Martina Wagner is the guide who will help you do it effortlessly, joyfully, and powerfully.

Her final words to the audience captured the essence of her message: "You are worth it. Your dreams are worth it. Step into your success—because you already have everything you need to make it happen."

This conversation wasn't just an interview; it was a masterclass in living a life of inspired choices. And for that, I am endlessly grateful.

Season 1, Episode 9, aired 12/14/2023
recorded 12/14/23 Amstetten, Austria / San Diego, CA, US

Connect with Martina: https://www.wagner-martina.com/

4.15 Creg Effs – Three Feet from Gold

Sitting down with Creg Effs always feels like a conversation with an old friend—warm, insightful, and brimming with inspiration. As an empowerment strategist, firefighter, author, and speaker, Creg embodies the strength and resilience he encourages in others. During this episode, he shared the profound experiences that have shaped his outlook on life, from the discipline required in his 22-year firefighting career to the wisdom he's gathered from his mentors—many of whom he's met through books rather than in person.

Creg's journey is a testament to overcoming adversity. "Never give up on your dreams," he said, his voice steady with conviction. "Even when obstacles appear, think of them as God's way of telling you to pause, rethink, and sometimes restrategize. But never stop moving forward." This perspective isn't just theoretical for Creg; it's the core of his message, deeply rooted in personal trials and triumphs.

One of the highlights of our conversation was his reflection on the book *Three Feet from Gold*. As Creg recounted, this book came into his life during a time of immense personal struggle. "I was at a crossroads, about to lose my marriage and feeling defeated," he shared. "Reading that book, it felt like the story was written about me. It taught me that often, people give up just when they're on the brink of success—only three feet away from gold."

Creg's story doesn't stop at resilience—it's about using that strength to empower others. Through his books, like *Everyone Deserves Love*, he offers lessons learned from heartbreak and self-discovery. "Love isn't just about emotions," he explained. "It's about understanding, patience, and aligning with what's truly meant for you. Even in brokenness, there's strength to be found."

Our discussion also touched on his work as a firefighter, a career that has profoundly shaped his character. "Being a firefighter taught me courage, empathy, and how to work with diverse personalities," Creg said. "It's not just about fighting fires—it's about building trust and showing up for others in their most vulnerable moments."

Beyond his professional accomplishments, Creg's humility shines through. When I asked about his mentors, he humbly mentioned that books have been his greatest teachers. From *Think and Grow Rich* to *How to Win Friends and Influence People*, he's drawn lessons from literary giants. "My mentors are in these pages," he said, "and they've shaped the person I am today."

One particularly touching moment was when Creg credited our shared community, the Suxess Club, for helping him launch his newsletter and gain confidence in his aspirations. "The support and constructive feedback from our group have been transformative," he said. "It's proof that when people lift each other up, amazing things happen."

Creg's vision for the future is equally inspiring. With plans to release a paperback version of his latest book and co-author a collection of poetry, he's constantly pushing his creative boundaries. And as he hinted at starting his own podcast, his passion for inspiring others seems boundless.

As our conversation drew to a close, Creg left us with a powerful reminder: "When you encounter obstacles, think of them as opportunities to pause and reassess. You might just be three feet away from your gold. Keep going."

This episode wasn't just a dialogue; it was a masterclass in resilience, love, and the power of never giving up. Creg Effs is proof that with the right mindset and support, we can all turn our struggles into stepping stones toward greatness.

Season 13, Episode 18, aired 5/1/2025
recorded 11/27/24 St. Thomas, Jamaica / Bavaria, Germany

Connect with Creg: https://sites.google.com/view/creginspires/
Everyone Deserves Love: https://amzn.to/4fYuVaM

4.16 Cherrian Angela Chin – Inspired by Nature

Meeting Cherrian Angela Chin for the first time was like stepping into a wellspring of wisdom and positivity. I remember our initial encounter through the Napoleon Hill Institute and how we later deepened our connection during a in-person event in Los Angeles. Cherrian embodies the very essence of inspiration, empowerment, and connection, and her story is one of remarkable growth and giving.

Cherrian shared her journey from Jamaica to the U.S., weaving in her experiences growing up in nature-rich environments. Her childhood in the serene mountains of Jamaica and later in the lush landscapes of upstate New York shaped her deep appreciation for natural beauty. She described how this love for nature became the foundation of her life philosophy and work. "Nature is my essence," she said, explaining how it fuels her creativity and empowers her to connect deeply with herself and others.

When she spoke about empowerment, Cherrian's passion was palpable. She reflected on how true empowerment isn't just about giving someone authority or a voice but helping them realize the strength and potential within themselves. She shared her experiences at Job Corps, where she works to provide students from disadvantaged backgrounds with the tools and skills they need to succeed. Yet, she acknowledged the paradox of empowerment: the opportunity to grow must be met with awareness, something not everyone is ready to embrace. Her ability to balance compassion with honesty allows her to guide others without judgment, encouraging them to rise above their circumstances.

Cherrian also explored the concept of inspiration and its many forms. For her, inspiration flows from various sources— books, music, art, and the voices of influential thinkers like Bob Proctor, Neville Goddard, and Peggy McColl. She shared a moving insight: "Even though most of them have transitioned, it feels like they're still here." This perspective highlighted her profound connection to the wisdom of the past and how it continues to shape her present. She spoke of how these figures, along with the beauty of the world around her, have propelled her toward growth and deeper self-realization.

Her thoughts on connection were equally profound. She described the invisible threads that bind us all and emphasized the importance of nurturing relationships that extend beyond surface-level interactions. "The world is smaller now," she noted, "but true connection still requires intention and effort." Her vision of connection goes beyond networking; it's about creating soulful bonds that inspire transformation and growth. She beautifully quoted Gina Bellman: "I love those connections that make this big whole old world feel like a little village."

Throughout her presentation at the *Stage of Inspiration* event, Cherrian seamlessly blended personal anecdotes with actionable insights. She reminded us of Napoleon Hill's words: "Strength and growth come only through continuous effort and struggle." Her journey, filled with challenges and lessons, exemplifies this truth. She shared how the ups and downs of life have shaped her, teaching her resilience and the importance of self-empowerment. "Imagine yourself as the best," she urged, encapsulating her message of embracing growth and striving for excellence.

Cherrian's authenticity shines through in everything she does. Whether she's empowering students at Job Corps, sharing wisdom from her favorite authors, or encouraging others to connect with the world around them, she leads with an open heart. Her commitment to living intentionally and inspiring others is a testament to her character and purpose.

For those seeking to connect with Cherrian, she offers a free Positive Intelligence (PQ) assessment—a valuable tool for understanding one's strengths and saboteurs. She invites listeners to reach out via Facebook or Instagram, where she continues to share her journey and inspire others.

I left our conversation with a renewed sense of purpose and a deep appreciation for the power of connection. Cherrian reminded me that inspiration, empowerment, and connection are not just abstract concepts; they are actions we can take every day to make the world a little brighter. Her story is a testament to the transformative power of living with intention and giving from the heart.

Season 1, Episode 13, aired 12/16/2023
Season 7, Episode 6, aired 8/8/2024

Connect with Cherrian: https://www.facebook.com/cherrianc/

4.17 Annie Boon – A Voice for Healing

Annie Boon's journey into the complexities of infidelity is nothing short of inspiring. Her candid and insightful conversation during our interview brought forth a new understanding of a topic often shrouded in silence and judgment. Annie, a mindset coach specializing in infidelity, passionately shares her experiences and the lessons she's learned, which now shape her work with women impacted by betrayal.

Her story begins in South Africa, where she has dedicated her life to helping mistresses and betrayed wives navigate the shame, fear, and despair that accompany infidelity. Annie's mission is clear: to be the calm in the storm, guiding you back to your North Star. She approaches her work with empathy, confidentiality, and a deep understanding of the emotional toll these experiences take.

During our conversation, Annie shared her journey into this line of work, which began with her own personal trials. Raised in a home where infidelity was a reality, she saw the damage it caused to her family, particularly to her mother. Despite vowing never to repeat those patterns, Annie found herself ensnared in an affair with a married man. The experience was devastating, leading to loss, shame, and a complete breakdown of her self-worth. But it was also transformative. With the support of her mother—a woman Annie describes as nonjudgmental, compassionate, and resilient—she began to rebuild her life.

Annie's personal experiences lend her a unique perspective. She understands the double shame a mistress carries: the stigma of the act itself and the sense of betrayal to other women. She also empathizes deeply with betrayed wives, who often internalize feelings of inadequacy and failure. Her work focuses on dismantling this shame through open conversation and support. She believes that shame loses its power when it is shared, and that the path to healing begins with speaking out.

One of the most moving parts of our discussion was Annie's insight into the role of conversation and connection. She emphasized the importance of having adult conversations about infidelity—honest, respectful dialogues that can provide clarity and even pave the way for healing. Annie encourages couples to address their struggles openly, even before issues arise, as a proactive measure. She shared how an honest conversation between herself and the ex-wife of the man she had been involved with ultimately brought peace and understanding to a painful situation.

Annie's advocacy extends beyond her coaching sessions. On her Facebook page, she shares anonymous letters from women affected by infidelity. These letters, written as cathartic expressions of pain and reflection, offer validation to others experiencing similar struggles. The overwhelmingly positive responses to these posts reaffirm Annie's belief in the power of shared stories to foster empathy and healing.

Looking ahead, Annie has ambitious goals. She dreams of bringing her message to a broader audience through podcasts, public speaking, and perhaps even a TED Talk. She aims to destigmatize conversations around infidelity, encouraging people to seek understanding before passing judgment. Her ultimate goal is to be a voice for those who feel they have none, providing support and hope to mistresses and betrayed wives alike.

Annie's work is not about condoning infidelity but about creating a safe space for those affected to heal. Her story is a testament to resilience, compassion, and the transformative power of vulnerability. In her words, "Shame cannot exist in the presence of light and conversation." Annie's light is one of understanding, courage, and unwavering commitment to helping others find their own.

Season 6, Episode 27, aired 7/16/2024
Season 7, Episode 13, aired 8/15/2024

Connect with Annie: https://www.syoufu.com/

4.18 Andy Paige – 100 Years of Inspiration

Sitting down with Andy Paige was nothing short of electric. Known for her charisma, entrepreneurial spirit, and passion for reinvention, Andy embodies the phrase "living life to the fullest." From her roles on iconic shows like *General Hospital* and *Starting Over* to creating the ingenious Girlie Go Garter, Andy's life is a testament to adaptability and vision. But what struck me most during our conversation wasn't just her career highlights—it was her unwavering commitment to a long and vibrant life.

When Andy shared her goal of becoming a centenarian, I was captivated. "I want to live to be 100," she said with palpable enthusiasm. "I've been dedicated to this idea for over 30 years, and it's why, at 54, I'm starting a whole new acting career." Her passion wasn't just about the years but about making those years count—thriving, learning, and evolving well into her golden decades.

Her dedication to longevity isn't just wishful thinking. It's a lifestyle choice rooted in intentionality. Andy spoke about the importance of staying relevant by embracing change and innovation. She reflected on how this mindset has shaped her life, from launching a product used in 85 countries to her latest endeavor as Pearl on *General Hospital*. "There's always something new to learn and grow from," she said, a sentiment that underscores her approach to life.

The idea of interviewing Andy when she turns 100 sparked an immediate promise between us. "That would be fantastic," she laughed. "You'll have to be around too!" The thought of celebrating her century milestone with another podcast episode felt as monumental as it was inspiring. For Andy, reaching 100 isn't just a goal—it's a declaration of her belief in the power of reinvention, resilience, and thriving at every stage of life.

Our conversation touched on more than just goals and entrepreneurship. Andy's perspective on happiness was a profound takeaway. "Happiness is the most attractive thing in the universe," she said. "The more happy you can make yourself, the happier world we all live in." Her words were a gentle reminder that the energy we bring to life has a ripple effect, shaping not only our experiences but also those of the people around us.

Andy's legacy continues to grow, both on and off the screen. As she collaborates with *General Hospital* to bring fictional products like Deception Beauty to life, she's proving that even a 61-year-old soap opera can innovate and evolve. Her ability to merge tradition with modernity is a reflection of her own adaptability and drive.

Reflecting on our conversation, I'm inspired not only by Andy's accomplishments but by her enduring optimism and commitment to making every day count. As I look forward to our promised interview when she turns 100, I'm reminded of the power of setting bold goals and living with intention. Andy Paige isn't just striving for longevity; she's crafting a legacy of inspiration, one year—and one inspired choice—at a time.

Season 9, Episode 16, aired 11/10/2024
recorded 9/23/2024 New York, NY, US / Bavaria, Germany

Connect with Andy: https://shophomeandheart.com/

Promise: Season 388, Episode 13, to be aired 7/4/2070
To be recorded by 7/4/2070, wherever we may be by then!

5. WHAT WORKED WELL: THE KEYS TO SUCCESS

When I reflect on my podcasting journey, it's clear that several key factors contributed to the success of *Inspired Choice Today*. From persistence and intuition to embracing the art of connection, these elements not only shaped my podcast but also transformed me as a person. Let me take you through what worked well and how these lessons can guide your own journey.

One of the most significant lessons I learned was the importance of connection. From the start, I wanted each episode to highlight my guest's expertise and unique story. I didn't know how many guests would say yes or how the process would unfold, but I followed my intuition—and the results were incredible. Out of 555 interviews, only five potential guests declined, and even then, I learned to separate their response from my ego.

The key? Showing up authentically, with all my imperfections and struggles. Being vulnerable helped me build trust with my guests and audience. It reminded me that we often create barriers for ourselves through limiting beliefs, and we hold the power to dismantle them through self-acceptance and transformation.

Feedback was another essential part of the journey. After one memorable interview, the guest suggested we exchange feedback on each other's performance. That moment, though rare, left a lasting impression. It taught me that asking for and offering constructive feedback is vital for growth.

Funny and unexpected moments also played a role. For example, I once scheduled an interview with a guest from Australia, only to have a different person show up. My initial confusion quickly turned into a great lesson in flexibility and going with the flow. It's these moments of surrender—allowing intuition to guide the process—that often lead to the most rewarding outcomes.

Recognizing milestones has been a key part of my success. Each step outside my comfort zone—whether it was asking someone to be a guest, recording an episode, or overcoming technical challenges—was worth celebrating. These moments remind us of the progress we've made and fuel us to keep going.

Every accomplishment starts in the mind. You make a decision, act on it, and then look back to see what you've achieved. It's important to acknowledge yourself for your bravery and persistence.

One of the greatest lessons I've learned is simple but powerful: **just ask**. Whether it's requesting an interview, asking for feedback, or seeking recommendations, you lose nothing by asking. The worst-case scenario is a "no," but even that can lead to valuable lessons.

Being coachable and open to advice from others also worked well. I studied successful podcasters, adapted strategies I admired, and applied Napoleon Hill's concept of synthetic imagination—taking existing ideas and improving them.

At its core, podcasting is about sharing what you're passionate about. I encourage you to find a topic that excites you—something you could talk about for days without losing interest.

Podcasting isn't just about producing episodes; it's about growth, connection, and making an impact.

6. THE ART OF INVITING PEOPLE

The art of inviting people is more than just reaching out; it's a transformative journey that begins within. As I reflect on my path, I realize how profoundly this process changed me—personally and professionally. When I first started my podcast, I had no idea how to approach potential guests, let alone invite them with confidence and clarity. But like everything else in life, growth comes through experience.

In the beginning, I reached out to my warm contacts—friends, colleagues, and acquaintances I had met throughout my journey in personal development. This felt like a natural step. After all, these were people I already knew and trusted. Their overwhelmingly positive responses gave me the initial momentum I needed. It was heartening to hear "yes" after "yes," and those first 50 episodes in 2023 came together with ease.

But then came the challenge: reaching beyond my immediate network. Inviting people I had never spoken to, never met in person, and often only knew through social media platforms like Facebook, Instagram, TikTok, or LinkedIn required a leap of faith. I crafted a simple, heartfelt invitation, asking, *"Would you love to be my next Inspired podcast guest?"* At the time, I didn't have a catalog of episodes to share or reviews to bolster my credibility. What I offered was trust—trust in the potential of the connection, trust in the process, and trust in the mutual value we could create together.

To my surprise, many said yes. This taught me an invaluable lesson: when you extend an invitation with sincerity and openness, it resonates. Of course, there were moments of rejection, and those were challenging. I had to look inward and ask myself, *Where am I not ready to receive? Where do I reject invitations in my life?* Addressing these internal barriers helped me grow, not just as a podcast host but as a person. And as I transformed, the frequency of "yeses" increased.

To refine my process, I explored new avenues to connect with potential guests. Platforms like Matchmaker.fm and Podmatch became essential tools. These spaces were filled with individuals actively seeking podcast opportunities, making the experience smoother and more aligned. Podmatch, in particular, felt like a game-changer—a community where both hosts and guests were fully invested in creating meaningful conversations.

But beyond tools and platforms, the true power of inviting people lies in the connections it fosters. Through my podcast, I've witnessed the mastermind principle in action—the idea that when two or more minds connect, they create something far greater than the sum of their parts. These conversations have not only enriched my podcast but also my life, reinforcing the idea that peace and change begin within and radiate outward.

The process of inviting guests became more than a logistical task; it became a workshop for personal growth. Reaching out required me to confront fears of rejection, echoes of childhood experiences, and the vulnerability of putting myself out there. But each invitation strengthened my resilience, honed my communication skills, and deepened my capacity for connection.

If there's one piece of advice I'd offer to anyone venturing into podcasting or any collaborative effort, it's this: embrace the art of inviting. Start small, with people you know, and expand outward as your confidence grows. Understand that every "no" is an opportunity for reflection and growth, not a personal failure. Trust the process and remember that this journey is as much about your transformation as it is about creating impactful content.

In the end, the art of inviting people is about choosing growth every day, stepping outside your comfort zone, and opening yourself to the infinite possibilities that come with connection. It's a practice, one you refine by doing. So, just start. Extend that first invitation, and let the journey begin. And if you ever need guidance or encouragement, know that I'm here to support you. Together, we can create something extraordinary.

7. BEHIND THE SCENES OF PODCASTING

Podcasting, for me, has been a journey of intuition, organization, and self-discovery. The process begins with a simple but profound question: how can I best serve my guest and audience? Prepping for each episode is less about rigid scripts and more about tuning into the energy of the guest. I ask myself what this person might need, and I seek guidance from intuition to craft the right approach.

Practically speaking, preparation revolves around a concise bio and a few well-thought-out questions. I rely on tools like ChatGPT to refine these bios and generate questions, keeping the process efficient and tailored. Scheduling is another key part of the prep work. I've set dedicated podcasting days— Thursday, for example—and optimized time slots to suit international guests, balancing my European time zone with their schedules.

Time zone awareness is vital, especially when working with a global audience. Flexibility is equally important. Guests may cancel or reschedule, and plans can shift unexpectedly. It's all part of the process, and adaptability becomes a skill honed over time.

On the post-production side, automation has been a game-changer. Moving to platforms like PodcastAI has streamlined editing and publishing, reducing the workload significantly. This innovation allows me to focus more on the creative aspects and less on technical hurdles. However, I recommend investing in such tools only when your podcast has grown into a sustainable endeavor. Start simple, reinvest your earnings wisely, and upgrade when it aligns with your vision.

Balancing workload has never felt like a challenge. Podcasting is a natural fit for me—a joyful expression of my passion for connection and storytelling. It doesn't feel like work because I've embraced it fully. Stepping outside my comfort zone has become second nature, and each episode feels like a step forward in mastery.

What I've learned most profoundly is that a podcast is an extension of its creator. You set the rules, the tone, and the vision. You're the star on your stage, and you choose how to engage with your audience and guests. By establishing clear standards and boundaries, you create a space that reflects your unique voice.

Behind the scenes, podcasting is about preparation, trust, and growth. But it's also about joy—sharing stories, connecting with incredible people, and creating something meaningful for yourself and others. It's your platform, your rules, your voice. And that's the beauty of it.

8. ENCOURAGEMENT FOR STARTERS

Starting your podcasting journey is a transformative step that begins with a simple but essential decision: What do you want podcasting to be for you? Is it a hobby, a potential career, or a platform to share your voice with the world? Once you decide, commitment and goal-setting become your guiding principles. Setting achievable goals, such as recording a specific number of episodes or inviting guests regularly, fosters self-discipline and builds confidence as you keep promises to yourself.

The most profound realization you may encounter is that your voice matters. Many people underestimate their unique gifts and talents, which are a combination of experiences and abilities only they possess. Sharing these gifts is not just a personal endeavor; it's a contribution to the world, a way to give back for the value others have shared with you. This realization carries a responsibility to act, to share, and to inspire.

For those just beginning, embrace the fun of discovery. If you need guidance, seek support. There's no shame in asking for help or learning as you go—everyone starts somewhere. The important thing is to start. Without trying, you'll never know if podcasting is for you. Taking that first step not only answers the question but also prevents future regret for paths left unexplored.

As with any new venture, challenges will arise, particularly the fear of rejection or criticism. Overcoming these fears starts with a shift in perspective: what others think of you is none of your business. The only opinion that truly matters is your own. You may stumble or search for words, and that's okay. Authenticity shines brighter than perfection. Podcasting is a journey of growth and self-improvement, and every misstep is a step forward.

Your voice has a unique impact, attracting people who resonate with your journey. Often, these listeners reflect your former self, seeking the guidance or inspiration you now offer. By taking one courageous step, you position yourself one step ahead, ready to light the path for others. This ripple effect of courage and connection is how you make a lasting impact.

As you navigate podcasting, embrace it as a space to improvise, improve, and inspire. Focus on positivity and avoid dwelling on problems, as negativity attracts the wrong energy and audience. Instead, embody courage and growth, becoming a beacon for others to take their next step.

Your podcast is more than a platform; it's a vessel for transformation—for yourself and your listeners. Step into this new field with faith and determination, knowing that every episode is a contribution to the light you share with the world.

Looking ahead, I find myself reflecting on this remarkable first year of podcasting and the connections it has brought into my life. If you were to ask me, was it worth it? My answer is an unequivocal yes. Every single day spent preparing, recording, and reaching out to guests has been a journey of profound connection. I've built relationships like never before, filling my phone with over a thousand contacts—a testament to the new life I've embraced through the art of connection.

Setting out with a goal of 1,111 episodes, I've already surpassed the halfway mark. Each milestone reminds me that this is only the beginning. Inspired by role models like the hosts of Next Level University, who have achieved nearly 2,000 episodes in just six years, I find myself dreaming even bigger. While I might reach my own 1,111 episodes in two years, I recognize that this is about more than just numbers—it's about continuing to listen to my inner voice and following where it leads.

As I look to year two, my goals remain ambitious yet rooted in passion. I'll aim to record as many interviews as I did in 2024, if not more, while deepening the impact of my work. Beyond the podcast, I envision a series of books documenting this ongoing journey. This first book is only the beginning of the *Inspired Choice Chronicles* series, and who knows what opportunities lie ahead?

Perhaps I'll take to the stage, honing my skills as a speaker addressing larger audiences. Or maybe I'll step into the realm of journalism, conducting in-person interviews with stars, musicians, or even everyday individuals on the street. The dream of hosting my own radio show still lingers, a playful yet compelling possibility that fuels my imagination. Timeframes don't concern me—whether this lasts a month, a year, or twenty years, as long as the passion remains, so will my commitment.

Looking forward, I see celebrations ahead—moments to honor the achievements of this journey, to gather in live events, and to spark panel discussions that amplify voices. I see myself helping others create their legacies through podcasts and books, encouraging them to embrace simplicity while delivering impact. With modest tools and unshakable passion, anyone can shine their light on the world, inspiring others to dream and realize their desires.

Volume 2 of this journey promises even more opportunities for collaboration. I'm excited to invite others to be part of the story, offering them a chance to contribute to the *Inspired Choice Chronicles*. This is about celebrating not just my journey but the collective power of connection, creativity, and shared purpose.

So here I stand, proud of this first book and the adventures it represents. To those reading, I encourage you to reach out. Let's start a conversation, build something meaningful together, and see where this journey takes us next. Thank you for being a part of this, and I can't wait to continue sharing this incredible adventure with you.

And by the way, the waiting list for Volume 2 is already open. Don't procrastinate—make your choice today!

10. RESOURCES AND WISDOM SHARED

Resources to start with (free versions)*

Spotify for Creators: free hosting and distribution
https://creators.spotify.com/

BeeKonnected: 60mins free videoconference per meeting
www.bit.ly/bkbillionaire

Calendly: schedule your guests
www.calendly.com

Resources for the advanced podcaster (paid options)*

PodMatch: find the perfect guest
https://bit.ly/podmatchinspires

PodcastAI.com
https://podcastai.com/

ModernIQs: get blog articles from transcripts in an instant
https://moderniqs.com/create-an-account/?res_aff=inspiredchoicetoday

---

* Some links may be affiliate links, which help support the growth and improvement of THE INSPIRED CHOICE TODAY

Wisdom Shared: Guiding Words from Guests

"Be here now."- The Amazing Soul

"Repetition is not repetition of reading, but repetition of use."- Troy R Chadwick

"Be the best version of yourself right here, right now at all times, and be consciously aware of that."- Brian Proctor

"If you came to me, that means you need some kind of support, and I am a servant."- Shawnti Refuge

"People don't like to be sold, but they love to buy."
- Jeffrey Gitomer

"If your present five minutes ago wasn't very good, start over. Begin again."- Brian Hite

"My success is absolutely guaranteed."- Laura Lee Kenny

"If you have an oil that doesn't smell good, you need it."
- Martina Wagner

"I found the meaning of true love."- Creg Effs

"Without connection, how can we grow?"- Cherrian A Chin

"We need to speak about it."- Annie Boon

"Our style should evolve as well."- Andy Paige

11. ACKNOWLEDGEMENTS

This chapter is dedicated to expressing my deepest gratitude to everyone who has been part of this incredible journey—the guests, listeners, and supporters who have made *The Inspired Choice Today* not just a podcast but a life-changing experience. Over the course of 365 days, I recorded 555 episodes. This journey has been nothing short of extraordinary, filled with unforgettable moments, heartfelt conversations, and the support of a community that continues to inspire me every day.

To my **guests**, thank you for sharing your stories, expertise, and insights. Together, we've created something truly special. From laughter to tears, we've built connections that extend far beyond the microphone. You are the heart of this podcast, and your willingness to show up and share your truth has been a gift to me and the listeners.

To my **listeners**, you are the foundation of this work. Knowing that each episode resonates with someone out there has fueled my persistence. You are the reason I kept going, even when the road was challenging. Your messages, feedback, and stories about how this podcast inspired you to start your own journeys have meant the world to me. This is for you— thank you for showing up, listening, and encouraging me to keep pushing forward.

To my **supporters**, those behind the scenes cheering me on, offering feedback, and lifting me up—I see you. You've been my pillars, giving me the strength to stay consistent, publish episodes every single day, and embrace every improvement along the way. Your encouragement reminded me of the higher purpose behind this work, and for that, I am endlessly grateful.

This journey is far from over. I promise you, there will be a second year. There will be more episodes—55, 555, even 1,111 episodes. The work continues because the message matters, and together, we're building something extraordinary.

To those who haven't started their podcasting journey yet, I want to encourage you: start today. You don't have to be perfect to begin. Everyone has a message that deserves to be heard. Trust me, the world is waiting for your voice.

Finally, a big shout-out to the nearly 10,000 people who have supported this podcast across all platforms, contributing to thousands of monthly listeners. I am deeply humbled and forever grateful for your trust, encouragement, and support.

This is just the beginning. I keep growing, listening, posting, publishing, and moving forward. Together, we are unstoppable. Thank you for being a part of this journey—I'll see you in the next chapter and, of course, in the next book.

With gratitude,
Caroline

12. ABOUT THE AUTHOR

Caroline Biesalski is a trailblazing *Inspired Choice Coach* and the host of the globally recognized podcast *Inspired Choice Today*, ranked among the top **5% of podcasts worldwide** on Listen Notes. Her journey is a testament to the transformative power of courage, persistence, and intuition. Once labeled shy and introverted, Caroline overcame social phobia and self-doubt to create a platform that inspires people worldwide to step into their fullest potential.

Caroline's passion for empowering others stems from her own life experiences. After years of navigating a career in accounting and business, she rediscovered her childhood dream of hosting a show. This dream, rooted in her love for storytelling and connection, ultimately became a reality when she launched *Inspired Choice Today*. Through her podcast, Caroline has interviewed hundreds of guests, sharing their wisdom and insights to inspire listeners to make bold, purposeful choices in their own lives.

As an *Inspired Choice Coach*, Caroline helps individuals transform self-limiting beliefs, align with their authentic selves, and take actionable steps toward achieving their dreams. She combines practical strategies with intuitive guidance, creating a unique approach that resonates deeply with her clients and audience alike.

Caroline's work is deeply influenced by principles from Bob Proctor's *Thinking into Results*, Napoleon Hill's *Laws of Success*, and her own lived experiences. Her ability to connect with people from all walks of life, paired with her authentic and relatable storytelling, has made her a sought-after coach, mentor, and speaker.

Today, Caroline continues to inspire and uplift through her podcast, coaching, and writing. Her mission is simple yet profound: to help others recognize the power of their choices, embrace their uniqueness, and create lives filled with meaning and purpose.

Caroline lives by the mantra that every great journey begins with one inspired choice—and she invites you to start yours today.

This is only the beginning.

- START NOW –

CHOICE

Authentic Stories, Surprising Lessons, and Practical Takeaways for Business Starters empowering you to make impactful choices for both your personal and professional life.

Listen to The Inspired Choice Today

www.podcast.inspiredchoice.today

Choose your platform: Apple Podcasts, Spotify, YouTube

Use the AI Chat to get answers about guests and topics

Become an inspiring interview guest by applying here

https://www.podmatch.com/hostdetailpreview/inspiredchoice

or send an E-Mail to interview@inspiredchoice.today

for any requests, feedback or further information about THE INSPIRED CHOICE COACHING with Caroline Biesalski

See you in the next adventurous chapter of your life!

Yours,
Caroline Biesalski
Inspired Choice Coach & Podcast Host